THE ART OF MAXIMIZING YOUR COMPENSATION

HOW TO NEGOTIATE A TOP PACKAGE AND GET EVERYTHING YOU DESERVE

LISA RANGEL

COPYRIGHT © 2024 Chameleon Resumes LLC

This document is intended for private, individual use only by the individual purchasing the document. Transmission, distribution, duplication or public use by any means (electronic, mechanical, recording, photocopying or otherwise) is prohibited without express written consent from Chameleon Resumes.

ISBNs:

Paperback: 978-1-7333176-9-6

Ebook: 979-8-9903948-0-3

DISCLAIMER: While the author has used her best efforts in preparing and producing this ebook, she makes no guarantees, representations or warranties with the respect to the accuracy or completeness of the contents of this book and specifically disclaim any implied warranties for sale for fitness for a particular purpose. No warranty may be created or extended through affiliate or marketing partnerships in print or online sales and marketing materials. The advice and strategies contained herein are the opinions and based off client experiences of the author and may not be suitable for your situation. You should consult with a proper professional where appropriate. The author shall not be liable for any loss of profit, income or commercial damages, including but not limited to special, incidental, consequential or any other damage.

CONTENTS

Why You Need To Negotiate ... v

1. Shifting Your Mindset ... 1
   from Past-Salary-Value to Job-Performed-Value
2. The Universal Rule ... 5
   for Determining Your Worth at Work
3. 13 Tactics to Negotiate a Pay Rise ... 7
   and Maximize your Salary
4. Negotiating an Executive Level Salary ... 15
   Believe you're worth the big bucks
5. Why Recruiters Ask For your Desired Salary Early On ... 19
   (And What to Do About It)
6. When Online Job Ads Request Salary Numbers ... 23
   4 Options to Consider
7. The One Bold Salary Negotiating Tactic ... 29
   Only High-Achievers Can Use
8. Negotiating Pay Rates ... 33
   for Contracting, Consulting, and Temporary Assignments
9. 10 Proven Tactics ... 39
   to Get Your Next Promotion Faster
10. Evaluating Your Offer ... 43
    Are You Really Getting a Raise?

Next Steps ... 49

About the Author ... 51
Also by Lisa Rangel ... 53

WHY YOU NEED TO NEGOTIATE

AND THE MESSAGE YOU SEND WHEN YOU DON'T

To negotiate your salary or not to negotiate... that is the question, for some. The answer is to *always* negotiate.

As a former recruiter, I found that candidates who negotiated gave the impression they valued themselves, appreciated their abilities, and knew their worth—and didn't want to settle for anything less than the compensation they believed they deserved.

On the other hand, if I saw candidates who couldn't give me a compensation range and didn't want to negotiate a salary, they seemed to me like people who didn't want to rock the boat and were simply grateful to be working at all.

Being grateful to have a job is a good feeling to have, of course. However, gratitude should not be a crutch or a guilt trip, nor should it push you to settle for less than the marketplace pays for your results, experience, and skills.

So negotiate for your salary. Be prepared to state an acceptable range. Be ready to present the evidence that shows why you are worth what you're asking for. And be primed to promote your achievements to give the strongest impression of your character and abilities, and optimize your compensation opportunity from the start.

This is the secret high achievers know:

They don't wait to be offered a great salary. They ask for it and present proof as to why it is warranted.

However, according to a *Harvard Business Review* article titled "How to Negotiate Your Next Salary" it can take about two years to renegotiate compensation. During that negotiation time, you lose financial ground.

In this book, you'll discover everything you need to negotiate a top salary and get compensated fairly for the work you do—without losing years of financial ground trying to do it.

Let's start with your mindset, because without a healthy mindset, nothing else I share in this book will make any difference at all.

CHAPTER 1
SHIFTING YOUR MINDSET
FROM PAST-SALARY-VALUE TO JOB-PERFORMED-VALUE

Some states in the United States have passed laws that prevent employers from asking for a candidate's previous salary. This type of legislation has been introduced to protect job seekers.

The idea is to help candidates who are underemployed for their skills to be able to right-size their salary and prevent prospective employers from underpaying. Future compensation will be based on the market value of the prospective job—not on the candidate's salary history, which may be vastly underpaid.

This has been hailed as progress by employee advocate groups. And it *is* progress for the job seeker.

But this legislation does not mean candidates can sit back and wait to be offered top salaries. It's crucial to shift your interviewing mindset from a past-salary view to a job-value view. It is up to you to promote yourself as the best candidate who deserves the best compensation by aligning your skills and results as evidence that you will excel in the role you're going for—and prove to the employer you're worth an above-average compensation package.

Beware of using this favorable legislation as an artificial prop to your salary negotiation. Just because an employer cannot ask about past salary, doesn't mean you're safe from being devalued based on past salary history.

Applicants are never safe from employers wanting to hire people at the best salary for them—*not* the highest salary the candidate wants.

Always be prepared to make your case. The responsibility to start a discussion to maximize your compensation lies with you.

Embrace these 6 simple mindset shifts and get into the headspace you need to negotiate the salary you want:

1. THINK OF SALARY NEGOTIATIONS AS BUSINESS TRANSACTION.

Too often, negotiations are seen as a one-sided power dynamic by candidates (and employers). But both you and the employer are investing time, skills, and resources into this relationship. You both have assets to bring to the table and, just like with any business deal, both parties expect to get value from the exchange. You're getting a job and opportunities; they're getting the best of your skills and experience.

2. KNOW YOUR WORTH BEFORE GOING IN.

This way, you can make a well-informed argument for the salary you want. Putting a dollar sign on your skills and experience can also help to boost your confidence during negotiations. You must understand your market value so spend time and effort researching industry standards and average salaries for your role and level of experience. Check sites like salary.com, payscale.com, and the Bureau of Labor Statistics to help you shed light on how much people who do what you do get paid. It'll also show you how salaries may vary depending on location and experience. We'll go into more detail about how to do this research later in the book.

3. CREATE YOUR HIGHLIGHT REEL.

Make a list of all your achievements, results, skills, qualifications, and contributions so you're able to prepare a compelling argument in favour of the salary you want. Plus, it's human nature to focus on our shortcomings; this exercise will remind you just how valuable you are, and why a prospective employer would be lucky to have you on the team.

4. CONSIDER THE EMPLOYER'S PERSPECTIVE.

Spend a little time thinking about the situation from the company's perspective—perhaps your immediate manager or the head of the division you'd be working in. What are their objectives and aims and how can you help them reach them? This gives you another way to think about how you can bring value to what they do.

5. EMBRACE OPENNESS AND HONESTY.

Come to your salary negotiations with clarity and openness. Clearly communicate your expectations, career goals, and the reasons behind the compensation you want. Ask the company about their expectations, too—and turn it into a constructive conversation.

6. BE PREPARED TO WALK AWAY.

Negotiations are about finding an agreement—but be prepared to walk away if the company's terms don't align with your needs or personal values, or don't reflect the value you could bring to the role. This crucial mindset shift is a strong one, showing that you're committed to getting a fair deal for yourself and the company.

These mindset shifts can take time to become permanent, so practice changing your thought patterns. And in the meantime, let's look at a universal rule for determining a person's worth at work...

CHAPTER 2
THE UNIVERSAL RULE
FOR DETERMINING YOUR WORTH AT WORK

One common misconception when negotiating salary is that raises are based on experience, length of time in the job, and demonstrations of past loyalty. While these factors can affect a decision to give a raise to a current employee, or a higher salary to a new hire, these are not the primary factors used by high-growth and performance-focused companies.

The bottom line for determining worth is this:

Does the employee make more money for the company than they cost the company?

That's it.

It may sound callous, but no one has a job out of charity any more. An employee keeps their job if they contribute more to profitability than their compensation costs—and higher salaries are offered only if the prospective hire shows they will bring a higher ROI (return on investment) to the company if they invest in their candidacy.

The company's ROI from hiring you is not necessarily

sales-related. For example, here are some ways employees can prove their worth:

- Able to attract top-tier, in-demand talent
- History of retaining high-performing employees
- Using skills to automate processes that lead to higher efficiency, lower costs, and increased profitability
- Introducing or improving best practices for cash management
- Discovering new markets or new ways to market existing products or services to create new profit streams
- Creating measurable goodwill that translates to profitability (long-term or short-term)

This list is not close to being complete... there are many other ways of demonstrating ROI to prove your worth as an employee. The key takeaway here is to know that you need to go into a negotiation with all the evidence you need to show a company what they can gain by investing in you—and what they will lose if they don't.

Do not go into a negotiation hoping seniority, loyalty, and long years of experience will automatically bring you the big bucks. Remember that Janet Jackson lyric, "What have you done for me lately?"

This is what all employers are asking before they offer a higher salary or give a raise. Give the company what they ask for and show them how your achievements transcend your expected job duties and responsibilities.

CHAPTER 3
13 TACTICS TO NEGOTIATE A PAY RISE
AND MAXIMIZE YOUR SALARY

Everyone needs to master the professional skills involved in asking for a raise, negotiating a salary increase stemming from a promotion, and maximizing a new job offer. When you ask for a raise, there are many things you can do in advance to increase your odds of landing the raise you want.

According to Payscale.com, the average annual salary increase hovered from 3 to 5 percent between 2012 and 2022. If you want to optimize your pay and maximize your raise, the following salary negotiation tactics can help—when done well:

1. PROVE YOURSELF BEFORE YOU ASK FOR A RAISE

Many employees ask for a raise but have not yet proven their value to the firm. View your potential raise as an investment made by the organization into you, so the company wants to see what their return on the investment made in you will be.

Place yourself in visible positions and promote yourself, your skills, and the activities you take on, to ensure decision-makers understand your value to the firm.

2. VOLUNTEER FOR A PROJECT CRITICAL TO THE COMPANY'S SUCCESS OR MISSION

One way to gain visibility is to offer your talents, time, and abilities on challenging projects that are relevant to the firm's success. You may find yourself working alongside key players within the company who can vouch for your work ethic and commitment to bring results.

3. RECORD YOUR PERFORMANCE— TRACK YOUR ACHIEVEMENTS

Do not assume your boss automatically knows what you've accomplished. Keep a log of all your successes and wins, no matter how big or small. This will help you make a compelling case for a raise, demonstrating your value to the company and justifying the firm's increased investment in you.

4. CAPITALIZE ON A RECENT, SIGNIFICANT SUCCESS

Have you just completed a project that went well? Diplomatically brag about yourself and your team's success to your boss and other critical decisions makers. If you don't promote yourself, no one will.

5. DO YOUR HOMEWORK—SEE WHAT YOUR PROFESSION IS WORTH

Using websites such as payscale.com, salary.com, the Bureau of Labor Statistics, and other industry-specific websites, find information about your profession and see if you are above, below, or at market rate for your skills and experience.

Use Perplexity.ai or an AI app of your choice to ask, "As a __ (position title) in __ (location), outline a compensation strategy to use in a negotiation. Include pay ranges and a list of perks and benefits to request." I like Perplexity.ai because it gives sources you can check before using the output.

If you are at or below what the market is paying and have significant successes under your belt, this could bolster your credentials and achievements and help you build a strong case for a pay rise.

6. TIE YOUR RAISE TO YOUR PERFORMANCE AND SUCCESS

Offer to lead a project and put your money where your mouth is—outline the parameters for success and propose linking a bonus or raise to meeting these parameters. For example, if your project were to streamline expenses or raise revenue, then receiving a piece of that financial success means your raise pays for itself.

7. LOOK AT OTHER OPTIONS BESIDES MONEY

If money is tight in the business, consider other forms of compensation regardless of your performance. This shows you to be flexible with your employer, while still allowing them to reward your contributions.

8. THINK, "WOULD I GIVE ME A RAISE?"

Be the person you would want to give a raise to. It's that simple.

Do you make your boss's job easier? Do you make your boss look good? Would they be excited to lobby for you to their managers to get approval to give you a raise? Do you make it worth the risk for them to stand up for you?

If so, think about how you can build a case with this in mind. If not, consider how you can make yourself indispensable to your boss—and start making it so.

9. BE A TOP 5% PERFORMER FOR YOUR EMPLOYER

If you are a Top 5% performer in your organization, the answer to "do I deserve a raise" would be "yes". If you did not receive the salary raise you were looking for this past year, pay attention to these last two points.

10. INVEST IN YOURSELF AND YOUR PROFESSIONAL DEVELOPMENT

When was the last time you furthered your professional education? Or attended an industry event? Companies want to invest in people who invest in themselves. Increasing your skills, qualifications, and knowledge demonstrates an ROI on the company's investment in your salary raise.

11. TIMING CAN BE EVERYTHING—ASK AT THE RIGHT TIME

Salary decisions and discussions often happen well before review time or fiscal year beginnings. Ask for a raise a quarter or two before the normal time raises are announced, to put yourself on their radar.

Avoid bad times to ask, such as when raises have already been announced (by then it's too late), or when poor financial reports come out (it's hard to justify further expense when times are harder).

Be sure to ask for an appointment with your boss to

have the discussion so you can be fully prepared. Do not try to wing it in an on-the-fly discussion.

12. ASK YOUR BOSS WHAT YOU CAN DO TO GET A RAISE NEXT YEAR

Did not get the raise you were hoping for? Allow your boss to be very candid with you about what you could do to improve your chances next year. Solicit specific feedback as to projects you could handle and ask for honest critiques on your performance to date.

Do not be defensive when receiving this information. It will help you improve so you can land a higher salary next year—take it in the spirit of professional development.

13. BE REALISTIC

No one wants to give a raise to someone who is asking for 65 percent, or who feels entitled to a raise. Those types of employees will never be happy, so companies do not invest their precious dollars with these people—don't be one of them.

Stick to a 5-25 percent range and have your documentation ready to make your case.

Whether you get what you want or not, be gracious, thank them for their time and consideration, and be grateful for what you have. Get feedback if things don't go your way, so you can plan to make the following year the best ever.

. . .

It's worth making a salary negotiation plan using these 13 points: look at timelines, and gauge how long it will take you to organise your arguments and evidence in favor of your raise. Treat it like a professional project and give yourself the best chance of success.

CHAPTER 4
NEGOTIATING AN EXECUTIVE LEVEL SALARY
BELIEVE YOU'RE WORTH THE BIG BUCKS

You got your foot in the door of that executive-level position you were eyeing, you nailed the interview, and you've been told you're at the top of the list of qualifying candidates. Congrats!

Then, the interviewer asks that dreaded question, "What kind of compensation are you looking for?"

Most job hunters tend to freeze up here, but for execs it can be particularly frightening. Big positions tend to equal big money—money a company is shelling out—so the stakes are higher for candidates seeking this kind of position.

In this chapter, you'll find some tips on negotiating an executive-level salary, as well as a few pointers on how to answer the interview question above.

BELIEVE YOU'RE WORTH THE BIG BUCKS

This may seem trite, but self-belief is one of the biggest issues people face when negotiating. If you want the big bucks you need to believe you deserve them—because if you don't believe you deserve it, how can you expect anyone else to?

You can't let yourself get bogged down by stories of the tanking economy, what the interviewer might think of you personally, what other candidates have said, or where the company may stand financially. The reality is, you don't know how much money the company has, where it wants to spend it, or what the interviewer is thinking. You also don't need to worry about what other candidates have said. The important thing to remember is why *you're* the right fit for the job and why your skills, experience, and potential merit the money you're asking for.

Keep in mind self-belief is very different from feeling entitled. Entitlement is comes from a place of control and privilege, whereas *believing* you deserve and can earn more money is just a healthy dose of self-esteem.

AIM HIGHER THAN THE MINIMUM SALARY YOU'LL ACCEPT

Most people will low-ball themselves at the first opportunity. They think they're being humble when in reality they could have made more money. Combat this by deciding on the *minimum* salary you'll accept—then answer their question with a *higher* figure.

The worst that could happen is they tell you it's not possible, at which point you begin negotiating. If this does happen then at least you know the offer probably won't go any lower than your minimum requirement.

With that being said, there does need to be a certain level of reality when talking about salaries. There's a big difference between asking for a 10 percent increase and asking for some extra zeros.

BACK UP YOUR SALARY NUMBER WITH EVIDENCE

Companies will pay good money for great candidates, so it's your job to show them you're a fantastic candidate and they need you on their team.

This starts even before they ask the salary question, so make sure to show your leadership qualities on your resume and during the interview.

You can really knock an interviewer's socks off by using quantitative examples. Tell them how you increased company revenue, brought down costs, blew sales numbers out of the water, or helped employees become more productive.

The more tangible proof you have to back up your examples, such as reports or performance reviews, the better your chances of getting the salary you want.

By providing hard evidence of your worth to the company, you also take care of any worries that the interviewer may think you're overreaching, overconfident, or that you sound conceited.

CHAPTER 5
WHY RECRUITERS ASK FOR YOUR DESIRED SALARY EARLY ON
(AND WHAT TO DO ABOUT IT)

You may have noticed on your job hunt that recruiters get down to business fast. In fact, you may be surprised that they ask a candidate about their desired salary right off the bat. The question may have even rubbed you the wrong way.

But this practice isn't going anywhere. In this chapter, you'll find out why—and how to handle the question when it comes up.

WHY RECRUITERS NEED TO ASK...

Not all candidates have realistic expectations. In fact, experience tells recruiters some candidates don't even live on the same planet when it comes to the compensation they're seeking.

If a candidate has totally unrealistic salary expectations, it's not worth the recruiter's trouble to bother with them. If nobody will pay that kind of salary, why go to the trouble of placing them? The recruiter's job is to look out for their clients' best interests, not send through unsuitable candidates who will waste everyone's time. A recruiter's client may be willing to negotiate, but only within reason.

You also have to consider things from the recruiter's perspective. If they don't ask a candidate about their salary, then pass that candidate along to their client, and the client discovers the candidate's expectations are unrealistic, that recruiter has just wasted the company's time. The client will make sure heads roll if the recruiter didn't ask the candidate upfront what their salary expectations were.

Recruiters get paid by the companies they recruit for, not by candidates, so they can't run that risk.

If you are an experienced candidate you should be paid at least market rate. If, for whatever reason, the proposed salary is below market rate, this is something you should explore during the interview.

WHY YOU SHOULDN'T BE OFFENDED...

Whenever you've needed a service from someone most people ask about rates early on in the process. In fact, money is usually the top concern. There's no need to fall in love with a service provider who is way above your budget; there are plenty of options out there.

Why should a salary be any different?

Remember: how you react and respond to the question is part of the interview. In other words, if you act offended, that tells the recruiter something about how you deal with situations that don't go as planned.

HOW TO ANSWER THE SALARY QUESTION...

If a recruiter asks what you were making at your previous job, there's nothing else to do but tell the truth. Hold your head up high and drop the number without excuses or apologies. It is what it is.

If they ask what salary you're looking for in your next role, answer with the salary range or total compensation you've been interviewing for.

Do not start with, "I want..." or "I'm looking for..."

Answer with, "I am interviewing for positions in the ___ to ___ range."

Answering in this manner does two things.

First, it lets them know you've got other companies calling you for positions at that pay rate (which always works in your favor when it comes to negotiating).

Second, this is a subtle way of letting them know the market thinks you're worth it (other companies are interested in working with you at that level).

If you haven't been called in for any interviews yet or you just started the job search, do some research and see what the going rate is for the position you're looking for. Then answer with the range the same way: confidently, based on your research and skill set.

Sometimes you have to fake it until you make it. (Confidence, I mean. Not skills and experience.)

CHAPTER 6
WHEN ONLINE JOB ADS REQUEST SALARY NUMBERS
4 OPTIONS TO CONSIDER

More and more online help-wanted ads are asking candidates to put in black-and-white their salary expectations—and it can be a source of uneasiness. Especially if they also require a salary history.

This is the new reality: recruiters are getting down to business fast because they do not want to waste time vetting applicants whose compensation requirements turn out to be beyond their—or their clients'—budgets.

The hiring process is expensive for everyone.

On the one hand, you might worry that your salary figure will be beyond what the job pays, which means your application will be tossed.

On the other hand, you might underprice yourself.

So, what's a candidate to do?

4 OPTIONS TO CONSIDER

In this turbulent marketplace for talent there are no longer absolute right answers. However, there are four options which successful job applicants can leverage to navigate and negotiate the compensation issue.

1. DO YOUR HOMEWORK

Before beginning a job search, look into compensation trends for the kinds of jobs you want to do in the type of company you want to approach. That includes conducting research on websites such as salary.com or payscale.com.

But don't simply conduct passive research; reach out to people in your network. Contact trusted colleagues and acquaintances on professional networks such as LinkedIn and ask about salary patterns.

If you did your due diligence comprehensively, you'll be able to calculate what level of salary you could request in various scenarios:

- Large companies, midsize or small businesses, and startups
- Enterprises known to be generous with compensation and businesses whose culture values frugality
- Successful companies flush with cash—and the bankrupt ones whose executive compensation is monitored by the courts

When it's a blind ad (i.e. the company is not identified), sift through the details to see if you can find clues about its size, culture, and finances to help with negotiation positions.

2. INSERT A "0" OR THE WORD "NEGOTIABLE," IF YOU CANNOT LEAVE THE FIELD BLANK

This is permissible, unless there is an explicit statement such as, "Applications not accepted without specific salary figure."

This tactic gives you time to learn more about the particular job on offer. If you wait, it's possible the company will put a number out there first, which is better for candidates. That's exactly what you want because you'll know immediately whether or not the salary is suitable for you, and may save you time and effort—or make sure the effort you're putting in is worth it.

That's the numbers part. The rest of your cover letter or "pitch" should present your strongest evidence as to why you are the best fit for the position. Quantify recent accomplishments similar to those you could achieve at this new company.

It's no longer enough to position yourself as capable of simply performing the job adequately. Companies are moving toward the lean model, which means every hire must create unique value.

To get recruiters' attention immediately, front-load that data in the email subject line and first few paragraphs. Use the phrase "the edge" to show recruiters you have a special something that other applicants may not have.

3. PROVIDE A SALARY RANGE

Remember that, just as in selling real estate, you can always go down but *never* up. Your range should not be too broad—you need to indicate to recruiters your general expectations. Narrow parameters such as $230,000 to $250,000 tell them you're ready to start a conversation about money.

Some experts believe using precise numbers such as "$233,500 to $245,500" signals that you've given serious thought to the calculation.

Now you've given the salary range, your pitch must explain in detail why you're worth that amount of money. In essence, you frame your past performance as evidence that you can achieve the results needed for this job—and do it better than the other applicants. A fundamental of game theory is that you anticipate competitor moves, then create your strategy to outmanoeuvre them.

For example, based on your experience or competitive intelligence, perhaps you expect other applicants will *only* play the innovation card. You do that too—but also highlight a track record in project management, which is "the edge" you're looking for.

4. FRAMING COMPENSATION HISTORY

Telling recruiters and potential employers what you've earned in the past can be a neutral issue, such as when your job search follows a traditional pattern. Positions you apply for offer at least a 10 percent increase on what you're earning now.

When you provide your salary history data, honesty is the best policy. Companies are likely to verify what you tell them by, for example, asking for your tax records.

The subject of previous compensation can become problematic when you're applying for positions which pay less than what you're earning now. For companies, this can be a red flag.

Will you bolt when a higher-paying job comes up? Will you be dissatisfied with the lower-paying job?

Here are four ways that may reassure recruiters you will be committed to the role, despite the lower salary:

1. Explain that you're trading off money to learn a new skill. Once you prove yourself, in several years, you hope to renegotiate compensation.
2. You understand the wage differences in this region versus your previous location.
3. Compensation consists of more than money. You value the company's culture and benefits.
4. Your family's financial situation has changed. You do not need as much money as before so you can now choose a job you love.

Focus on selling yourself and the value you bring to the role, not just the bare numbers.

Beware, though: dealing with the numbers so early in

the job-search process can distract you, so stay focused on the purpose of the application and interview: **to sell yourself.**

Persuasive cover letters can motivate recruiters to offer you more than they or you might have planned. Nothing, especially compensation ranges for executive positions, is cast in stone.

CHAPTER 7
THE ONE BOLD SALARY NEGOTIATING TACTIC
ONLY HIGH-ACHIEVERS CAN USE

Many popular job search coaches advise executives to hold out during a salary negotiation and *not* give a range when asked. This is great in an ideal world... and in reality, it works occasionally.

But I can tell you first-hand, as a recruiter, that many executive candidates I interviewed did not move onto the next step if they didn't give me a salary range.

This is how that conversation between my recruiter-self and the executive job seeker would go:

Me: What salary range are you seeking?

Job seeker: Well, I'm sure you will compensate in the right range for the talent you want.

Me: Well, what is the salary range you're looking for?

Job seeker: Let's see where our conversation goes and we can determine what's fair at the offer stage.

Me: Well, can you give us an indication?

Job Seeker: Well, what is your budget Mr Employer?

Me: We expect to pay fairly for the most qualified

talent. We don't want to move forward unless we know we are all on the same page in the same range. Can you give us an indication of the salary ranges of the positions you're interviewing for?

Job Seeker: I prefer to keep chatting to learn more about the position.

Me: I understand. I know there are numbers candidates will not go below and numbers they would get excited about, but if you prefer to not offer that information, I understand. Let's continue.

This conversation can go on and on, if allowed to do so, and at this point, I would ask other questions to see if the candidate had enough proof to overcome the red flag indicated by their polite decline of the politely asked salary question. Most didn't have that proof. So I'd end the interview and the candidate did not move forward in the process.

Why?

Because I was not willing to be burned by someone saying they were in the ball park, getting to the final interview, then coming in with a range that was completely out of whack with what their skills warranted. This happened to me early on in my recruiting career and my company client was angry with me for wasting their time, having to start over, and setting their search back by weeks. The candidate who assured me he was "within a reasonable range" was not even close to the above market range my client was willing to pay.

Once burned, twice shy. This is why recruiters press

for the desired salary number—some of your fellow job seekers ruined it for you.

So, what is the one bold salary negotiating tactic only high-achievers can use?

BE PREPARED TO BOLDLY STATE A COMPENSATION RANGE FIRST

By now, most savvy executives on either side of the recruiting desk know the age-old negotiating tactic of "whoever says the first number loses." Sometimes this game is played at an interview ad nauseam, as demonstrated in the above sample conversation.

So unless an executive job seeker is prepared to be shown the door when pressed by some recruiters for a range, I say be prepared with a range. Say it boldly and confidently.

Being prepared with a range rather than deflecting the salary discussion is a tactic used by resilient executives prepared for all scenarios. However, this is not a tactic for the timid or bottom rung of performers. You need to have the achievements and the gravitas to pull it off.

CHAPTER 8
NEGOTIATING PAY RATES
FOR CONTRACTING, CONSULTING, AND TEMPORARY ASSIGNMENTS

Having run a consulting recruiting practice, I've found there is a special level of commitment to roles from consultants, contractors, and temporary employees. Here's why:

- When these interim employees give their word and commit to an awkward-length short-term assignment, their long-term job search is often sacrificed so they can remain committed to their current assignment.
- Because their career-advancement interviewing falls by the wayside, if their assignment ends abruptly, they often do not have another job lined up—because they haven't been interviewing. So they find another temporary assignment to fill the gap... and so on. This starts what I call the "temp rut," when someone becomes trapped in one interim assignment after another, because

they have to take *something* to earn money, but because of those temp positions, their interviewing is erratic and inconsistent.
- When a job seeker has a "temp rut" history, a recruiter or hiring manager often sees them as "jumpy." But I find the exact opposite to be true—these employees stick to the end of an assignment, even if their own long-term career is damaged because of it. They are a very loyal bunch, typically.
- Interim employees have a tendency to put the job before themselves. If they did put themselves before their current job, they would pursue the stability and rich benefits found with a direct hire job. There are exceptions to this observation, of course, but this is my experience working with long-term, interim-assignment employees.

It is important, even paramount, for consultants to use these positive attributes in their interviews and negotiations, to make the hiring manager aware of their value, so they can maximize their pay rate. Most HR professionals, recruiters, and hiring managers are unaware of the unique traits contractors bring to the table, unless they've dealt with placing contractors directly, which I have.

HOW TO CALCULATE THE CONTRACTOR PAY RATE

Use this calculation as a basis for coming up with your contractor rate to begin your negotiation:

- Start with how much you want to make per year. For example, let's use a target income of $75,000.
- Take that figure and divide it by 2,080 hours, which is a 40-hour week multiplied by 52 weeks. For our example, it would look like this: $75,000 / 2,080 = $36/hr hourly rate.
- If this is what you want to settle on, do not start with this hourly rate. Increase your starting figure, so when you negotiate and come down a bit, you'll end up at the rate that satisfies you.
- You may also want to factor in the monetary value of benefits and perks normally found in a direct hire job that you do not get in a contractor position, if your contractor role is tricky to fill.

CONSIDER THE UNIQUE CHARACTERISTIC OF THE CONSULTING/CONTRACTOR WORK STRUCTURE

Negotiate contractor pay rates differently than direct hire compensation packages. It is not the same discussion and a job seeker needs to be properly prepared for this type of negotiation.

Not only do unique skills and evidence of results factor into the pay discussion, as with a direct hire negotiation, you need to factor into to the contract arrangement the characteristics of what make a consultant a consultant.

Some factors that can favorably affect the pay rate:

- Short-term assignments are often harder to fill with top talent and can occasionally require higher pay, based on supply and demand.
- The skills needed for the contract assignment are not readily available in the contract candidate labor pool, warranting a higher pay rate.
- The position requires a long commute, frequent travel, or relocation. Road warrior contractors often need a premium rate to accept a position and relocations will also command a higher pay rate.
- The pay rate may also have to reflect the candidate pulling themselves out of the labor pool to take the assignment, if the assignment is an unpopular length and the skill set is rare.
- If benefits are not included and the candidate will have to pay for their own benefits, this may need to be factored in for a competitive candidate.

Conversely, there are points that can adversely affect pay rate negotiations. A job seeker must be prepared to counter these:

- Long-term unemployment gaps.
- Benefits included in the candidate's compensation will lower the pay rate, as benefits are a desirable perk.
- The more a contract position reflects a direct hire role, the less likely a higher-than-normal pay rate is warranted, as more candidate prefer stable employment. The same assumption can be made if it is known from the start that a contract role is very likely to turn into a direct hire role.

When you're negotiating pay rates for a contracting, consulting, or temporary assignment, keep all these points in mind—and make sure you use your knowledge to negotiate the best rate you can.

CHAPTER 9
10 PROVEN TACTICS
TO GET YOUR NEXT PROMOTION FASTER

Do you know how to avoid getting overlooked for a promotion? When the opportunity for promotion presents itself, it's important to make the most of it.

These 10 tips will put you on the right path and help you get your next promotion faster, by highlighting strategies such as being proactive, displaying strong initiative to decision makers, and showcasing your leadership qualities.

1. DO THE JOB YOU WANT FIRST, THEN GET IT

Throughout my career, this has been my promotion philosophy: I always started doing the job above me *before* I was promoted into it. I never undermined my boss, but when it came time for my boss to be promoted, it made my boss's promotion come easier knowing I was there to step into their job seamlessly.

2. TAKE INITIATIVE

Don't wait for things to happen. Said another way... *Go make stuff happen.* Don't always wait for permission, either. Sometimes asking for forgiveness is the right path as it means you got something done.

3. SELECT A DEPARTMENT THAT WILL SHOWCASE YOUR STRENGTHS

Don't be a salmon swimming upstream, unless you actually like fighting with management all the time. Find a profession and a culture that complements your work style so you shine and accelerate faster.

4. MAKE YOUR BOSS'S PRIORITIES YOUR PRIORITIES

Know your boss's goals and do the work to support them. Period.

5. MAKE YOUR BOSS LOOK GOOD

Promote your boss's achievements. Be an awesome subordinate (whether or not your boss contributes to your success). Often, if your boss knows you have their back, they will promote you with them as they rise in the organisation.

6. TRAIN OR MENTOR OTHERS WITHOUT BEING ASKED

When the organisation is looking for people with experience to bring others up through the ranks, if you've mentored people without being asked, you can say you have that experience—and demonstrate it. This goes back to doing the job you want, then getting it.

7. BE THE GO-TO PERSON EVERYONE LIKES TO WORK WITH TO GET STUFF DONE ON CHALLENGING PROJECTS

Who is the person in your department or company people go to for answers and to get things done? If it's not you, you have work to do.

8. FIX CRITICAL ISSUES NOBODY ELSE WANTS TO TACKLE

Be the hero. Simple as that…

9. DON'T LOSE SIGHT OF THE LONG-TERM STRATEGY WHILE WORKING ON SHORT-TERM PROJECTS

Showcase your ability to look long-term to demonstrate you have strategic vision. Don't get lost in the short-term details or you can get pegged as a good doer rather than a good leader.

If your goal is to lead, you need to show yourself to be

an effective leader—which means keeping an eye on the future.

10. PRIORITIZE YOUR ASCENT

Don't leave promotions to chance. Nobody will promote you if you're simply waiting to be picked. Make time to develop your skills. Ask decision-makers what it takes to get promoted, and make a plan to do that. Don't wait to be chosen: ensure you're the clear choice when the time arises.

Part of prioritizing your ascent is having your resume ready, your profile updated, and your network primed and ready to help you.

If you haven't already, you should definitely check out my book *The 6-Figure Resume*, which will help you do this.

Build these 10 proven tactics into your raise plan, and start implementing it right away.

CHAPTER 10
EVALUATING YOUR OFFER
ARE YOU REALLY GETTING A RAISE?

There you are, sitting with your new promotion or new job offer, bursting with excitement! As everything seemed to go well and you're so excited, it's easy to breeze through the acceptance phase because (a) you want to be done with this long arduous process and (2) you believe the company acted in good faith and presented you what seems to be a fair offer at first glance.

However, this is the exact time you need to be vigilant. Be thorough right to the end of the process—the end of the process being the day you start your new job.

Evaluating your offer is as crucial to landing the *right* job as is preparing for an interview or writing an effective resume. So don't lose your focus at this critical stage.

It's imperative to evaluate each component of an offer and compare it to your current role. Consider what you're expecting as compensation based on your research of what the market pays for the job you do. Do not leave this to chance or assume the prospective employer will structure the deal favorably for you.

Your new employer will almost certainly not purposefully try to pull one over on you; after all, that wouldn't be a good way to start a new hire. However, what an employer may offer in good faith, thinking it's better than what you currently earn, may not in reality be better than your current circumstances. The only way you will know is if you personally do the comparison.

Here's a guide to help you, but this list is by no means exhaustive.

SALARY & MONETARY COMPENSATION

- Is your bonus going to be higher than the one you receive now? Is the basis for bonus calculation going to enable you to actually achieve and receive the bonus?
- Will your tax structure change because of a salary increase or location change?
- When are you reviewed as an employee? Is it as often as you are reviewed now, or less? If it's less often, that could mean less frequent raises.
- How about profit-sharing?
- Are 401(k) plans offered with a match?
- Is there a pension?
- What are the long- and short-term incentives (LTI and STI)?

Could the existence of any of these perks outweigh any portion of the offer that is lacking?

HEALTHCARE BENEFITS

This category is where major compensation discrepancies can occur.

- What are the premium payments—are they more or less than what you currently pay?
- What carrier is offered?
- What is the plan's reputation in terms of being accepted by quality healthcare providers?
- Are your current doctors included in the new plan?
- What will be the potential differential in out-of-pocket expenses pertaining to labs, specialists, and other medical services?
- Is there an executive wellness plan?

WORK ARRANGEMENTS

Are you offered flextime or work from home agreements?

These arrangements can save money if you can dress casually (less money spent on professional attire and upkeep) and commuting or child care costs. It can also improve quality of life, which may be hard to put a price on, but can make you more flexible about the offer if the money is less than you expected.

VACATION

Are you being offered more or less time off? What format does your vacation time take—is it PTO, vacation—and how about sick pay?

COMMUTE/LOCATION/TRANSPORTATION

Be sure your commute is shorter or similar to what you do now and that it costs the same or less. Remember, adding 30 minutes to your commute adds at least *five hours* per week to your work day, so reduces your hourly pay rate. Unless you have a significant pay raise to justify a longer commute, you may, in effect, be taking less money by having a longer commute.

Does your new employer offer reimbursable or discounted transportation perks?

TUITION REIMBURSEMENT & PROFESSIONAL DEVELOPMENT

Any costs picked up by your new employer should be compared to what you have now. Other components to factor into your offer evaluation:

- Childcare services
- Title/office arrangement
- Relocation covered/not covered
- Expense account
- Company car
- Gym membership and wellness perks

It is imperative to put a monetary and intrinsic amount to each part of the new offer and compare it to what you had/have in your previous/current role, to determine if this new offer is truly better.

Don't assume it is. Do the work to come to that conclusion definitively.

NEXT STEPS

Everything you need to give yourself the best chance of negotiating the best salary and compensation package is right here in this book.

If you only take one message away, let it be this:

The highest paid executives don't wait to be offered a great salary. They ask for it and present proof as to why it is warranted.

Remember: those who sit back and wait to be recognised will be waiting for a very long time. It's up to you to figure out what you believe you're worth in a new role—and put together a plan to make it happen.

It can feel like an overwhelming task, but you don't have to do it alone. Want us to personally help you negotiate a higher salary?

Hire us here:

http://chameleonresumes.com/interview-mastery-system

Our Interview Mastery System covers how to

maximize your salary through compensation negotiation tactics used only by high-achievers.

Have a question? Reach out to me here:

Lisa Rangel
lr@chameleonresumes.com
www.chameleonresumes.com

ABOUT THE AUTHOR

Lisa Rangel is the founder and managing director of Chameleon Resumes, named a Forbes Top 100 Career Website. She was a moderator of LinkedIn premium groups and career blogger for 8 years. As a recruitment professional for 13 years and as a Cornell University graduate, Lisa has held management and producer roles in numerous companies, ranging from international recruitment conglomerates to focused executive search firms.

In Chameleon Resumes, she has assembled the best team of resume writers and job search consultants who all have prior search firm and corporate recruiting experience — Chameleon is the only firm of its kind! Lisa and her team know first hand which resumes get a response. They've reviewed thousands of resumes over the years and helped top recruiters and talent for top organizations, working with clients in 88 countries.

Lisa is a member of the National Resume Writers' Association and Professional Association of Resume Writers and Career Coaches. She has been featured in person, online and in print on Fast Company, Forbes, LinkedIn, Newsweek, Money, Business Insider, CNBC, BBC, Crain's New York, Chicago Tribune, CIO Magazine, American Marketing Association, eFinancial Careers,

The Vault, Monster, U.S. News & World Report, Good Morning America, Fox Business News and many other reputable publications.

She is the author of nine books, creator of the Get Hired Fast job-landing training series at JobLandingAcademy.com, and a serial advice giver through her website ChameleonResumes.com. You can sign up to get advice from Lisa directly into your inbox from:

https://chameleonresumes.com/get-daily-career-tips/

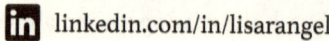 linkedin.com/in/lisarangel

ALSO BY LISA RANGEL

The Job Landing Mindset

The 6-Figure Resume

Cover Letter E-Notes: The Modern Way to Land Interviews

7 Job Landing Steps to Find a Role that Makes You Happy

Interview Powerfully

www.ingramcontent.com/pod-product-compliance
Lightning Source LLC
Chambersburg PA
CBHW030535080526
44585CB00014B/958